W9-CPF-804

Communion
Handbook

Communion Handbook

Paul E. Cook

Judson Press® Valley Forge

Communion Handbook

Unless otherwise indicated, Bible quotations in this volume are from *The Holy Bible,* King James Version.

Other versions of the Bible quoted in this book are:

The Revised Standard Version of the Bible, copyrighted 1946, 1952, 1971, 1973 © by the Division of Christian Education of the National Council of the Churches of Christ in the United States of America. Used by permission.

The American Standard Version, copyright © Thomas Nelson & Sons, 1901.

Library of Congress Cataloging in Publication Data

Cook, Paul E.
    Communion handbook.

    1. Lord's Supper (Liturgy)—Handbooks, manuals, etc.
I. Title.
BV825.5.C67   264'.36   80-14202
ISBN 0-8170-0877-2

The name JUDSON PRESS is registered as a trademark in the U.S. Patent Office. Printed in the U.S.A. ⊕

PREFACE

I t is my hope that church leaders will find the contents of this book helpful in making the Communion service more interesting for congregations. The material will be particularly helpful to congregations in the free and independent traditions. I feel churches of the free tradition have more opportunity than liturgical churches to exercise flexibility and make the Communion service interesting and even exciting. I hope what I share herein will spark other ideas and innovations. Our vast legacy of words of Scripture, prayers, and praise should be ever enriching our experience of the Supper.

I have tried with a great deal of effort to trace the material to its origin. In some cases I'm sure I have failed. I am deeply grateful to every source, known and acknowledged, as well as to those unknown. I especially appreciate the help of a tireless secretary, Mrs. Ann Ravis, the technical help of Professors Barbara Smith and Debra Wynn, two outstanding congregations, one in Newark, Delaware, and one in Philippi, West Virginia, and to the folks at Judson Press.

In memory of
our Savior's love,
PAUL E. COOK

TABLE OF CONTENTS

INTRODUCTION 9
1 THE SUPPER 11
2 BASIC OUTLINES AND VARIATIONS
  OF THE COMMUNION SERVICE 15
3 SPECIAL COMMUNION TIMES 25
4 COMMUNION SERVICES WITH THEMES ... 51
5 SERVICE RESOURCES 61
6 OTHER INNOVATIONS 89
  NOTES 95

INTRODUCTION

As a pastor I have often been dismayed as I have witnessed people leaving the church because they noted that Communion was to be served. The Communion service is all too frequently a "ho-hum" affair that has not been altered in years. Yet Communion can be the most dramatic and exciting service of worship we have if we are flexible and do some planning.

This sacred feast is each minister's high privilege and yet one of the most important, oft-recurring, and exacting services of worship. Because of the frequency and importance of the Communion service, the procedures and resources in this book are being shared. No service deserves more careful planning in order to keep it fresh, dramatic, and useful for our congregations.

The Communion observance should not be hampered by precise rules and procedures. There is something alive in the observance, and it can be expressed and appreciated in many ways. The real presence and experience of Christ is fundamental to the service. Prayer, meditation, offerings, participation, music, and fellowship can be framed into a service that will communicate Him.

I sincerely hope the ideas and material shared here will help busy ministers in this regard.

THE SUPPER

For almost two thousand years Christians have assembled to eat and drink the elements of the Lord's Supper. This observance has undergone many changes. More variations exist today perhaps than ever. In magnificent buildings with men dressed in elaborate vestments the distribution of the Communion is very solemnly and even pompously made. But at a summer camp, junior high youth may, by using soft drinks and crackers in the midst of glad informality, convey the same sense of commemoration of the first Supper and remember Jesus Christ.

Ways of observing the Supper have changed because of the variety of cultures and people who have adapted it as part of their worship experience. But Christians down through the centuries have been concerned to continue the observance which Jesus instituted.

Many names have been attached to the observance. "Communion" is suggested by the instruction of the Scriptures to participate in the body and the blood. Mark 14:23 suggests the reference of "Eucharist," the giving of thanks. The term "mystery" was used sometimes to refer to something hidden or secret, but other times it was used to refer to something that had been hidden but now was made clear by God.

During the fourth century the term "Mass" was used to refer to the Supper. The Roman Catholic Church still applies it.[1]

Interpretations

As Christians have developed varieties of ways to observe the Supper, so also we have evolved a variety of understandings and interpretations.

Some branches of the Christian family interpret the Supper in terms of sacrifice. "Sacrifice" and "offering" have been terms used since the beginning. The Roman Catholics teach that the bread and the wine are changed into Jesus' body and blood. The priest, in behalf of the people, offers the bread and wine as propitiation for sins.

Another major interpretation has been that the Supper is observed in terms of a memorial rather than sacrifice. Some believers have insisted that the bread and the cup are symbols of Jesus' body and blood. The service is commemorative and reminds us that Jesus gave his life for our salvation.

A third interpretation of the Supper is in terms of what God does for us when we in sincerity and understanding receive the bread and the wine. In this interpretation Christ is present in the observance, and he is received by the participants.

But whether the observance is called sacrament or ordinance, whether the bread and wine are changed miraculously, whether the cup is wine, juice, or soft drinks, or the bread is unleavened or a cracker, the Supper is a bond of union between the branches of Christianity.

There is one bread, one cup, one Christ, and truly one fellowship and brotherhood.

We celebrate the living Christ and the church's identity with him. It is a joyful feast, not a mournful fast. The Supper reminds us of all Christ has done and is doing for us. We celebrate the victory we share in him and our eternal hope.

Making the Supper a Memorable Occasion

A church must try hard to make the Lord's Supper a service to remember. Perhaps most Protestant churches have the Supper once a month, with special observances during Holy Week, Advent or Christmas, retreats, and other very special times.

The Lord's Supper should be the central focus of the service. Hymns, prayers, and other parts of the service should reinforce the dramatic message the Supper proclaims. The service should have a special order with a variety of material; each month's service should not be a repeat of the previous month's. The service should not be added or tacked on to a regular service, keeping the people in church beyond the normal time period.

Variety can be expressed in almost all phases of the service, including the types of bread, use of juice and wine, methods of distribution and participation. Music should be a vital part of the Communion itself. The congregation can sing or listen to appropriate music as part of their participation.

Prayer is an integral part also. Confession is a vital element to this observance. Written confessions can be utilized, or a corporate confession can be read in unison. Words of assurance confirmed by the Communion message are to be given. Sometimes silence is a key in making the Supper memorable.

We can look at our congregation, study their needs, and determine whether our Communion services meet any of these needs. We can determine whether the service helps people meet God.

BASIC OUTLINES
AND VARIATIONS OF THE
COMMUNION SERVICE

The Communion service can be observed in the first part of the service very effectively, or it can be placed in the middle part of the worship hour and be the focal point of the entire worship time, or it can be the highlight and the climax of the service when placed at the end of the service concluding in silence or with a hymn of devotion. Most all free churches will include the following basic parts of the Communion observance:

> Words of Invitation
> Words of Institution
> The Bread:
>   Prayers   Distribution   Participation
> The Cup:
>   Prayers   Distribution   Participation
> Concluding Words
> Hymns, Prayers, Statements of Faith, etc., are to be inserted where appropriate.

The sermon or meditation for the day can be before, after, or a part of the Communion, or sometimes there can be an observance without any sermon at all. Invitation words can be called "humble access words," etc.

In the following sections of this chapter are resources for use in the outline above.

A

In the following outline the prayers are arranged differently than in the previous outline.

Words of Invitation
Pre-Communion Prayer (*or prayer of humility*)
Hymn
Words of Institution
The Bread: Distribution   Participation
The Cup: Distribution   Participation
Post-Communion Prayer (*or prayer of dedication*)
Hymn

B

The following service introduces a memorial service as part of the Communion. Names of members who have died are read, followed by Scripture and prayer.

Words of Invitation
Pre-Communion Prayer
Hymn
Words of Institution
The Bread: Serving   Participating
Silent Prayer Period
The Cup: Serving   Participating
Post-Communion Prayer
Memorial Service
Hymn

C

More participation by the congregation is called for

in still another type of service. The people sing together the hymns, say the Lord's Prayer, and in unison read the Words of Institution.

Words of Invitation
Communion Hymn
Words of Institution (*in unison*)

> "And as they were eating, he took bread, and blessed, and broke it, and gave it to them, and said, 'Take; this is my body.' And he took a cup, and when he had given thanks he gave it to them, and they all drank of it. And he said to them, 'This is my blood of the covenant, which is poured out for many. Truly I say to you, I shall not drink again of the fruit of the vine until that day when I drink it new in the kingdom of God.'
>
> "And when they had sung a hymn, they went out to the Mount of Olives" (Mark 14:22-26, RSV).

The Lord's Prayer
The Bread:
    Prayer   Distribution   Participation
The Cup:
    Prayer   Distribution   Participation
Concluding Hymn

D

In still another service the instructions are printed in detail, giving people a sense of participating in the drama.

Invitation to the Communion
Hymn for Communion
Opening Communion Sentences
Words of Institution for the Bread

> (*The pastor will take the bread, break it, and say, "*. . . This is my body which is broken for you . . ." [1 Corinthians 11:24]. *Then he will hand the plates to the servers, who will hold them during the prayer.*)

Prayer of Thanksgiving for the Bread (lay person)
Words of Institution for the Cup

> (*The pastor will take in hand a cup or tray of cups and say:* "This cup is the new covenant in my blood" (1 Corinthians 11:25, RSV). *Then the servers will lift them up in the prayer of thanksgiving.*)

Prayer of Thanksgiving for the Cup (lay person)
Communion Hymn
The Lord's Prayer
Invitation to Participate

> (*The servers will now proceed to give the bread and the cup to the people, passing the plates and the trays to the congregation in a reverent manner. The people will be instructed to consume the elements as they are ready to do so.*)

Concluding Sentences

E

The following service incorporates more formal participation. The Confession of Sins may be placed at the beginning of the service. Instructions are to be given the people to consume the elements as they are ready.

The Confession of Sins

"Let us draw near with a true heart, and confess our sins unto God our Father, beseeching him, in the name of our Lord Jesus Christ to grant us forgiveness."[1]

(Let the congregation silently pray.)

"Gracious God, you have promised to receive us when we come to you; we confess that we have sinned against you in thought, word, and deed. We have disobeyed your law and failed to love our neighbors. Forgive us, free us from sin, and grant that we may live and serve you in newness of life; through Jesus Christ."[2]

The Service of Holy Communion

Words of Welcome

Prayer of Thanksgiving

The pastor breaks the bread and says, "The bread which we break is the body of Christ."

The pastor pours the cup and says, "The cup we bless is the blood of Christ."

Then the pastor says, "Come, for all things are ready."

The bread and the cup are distributed and those receiving say as they consume, "The body of our Lord Jesus Christ, the bread of life. The blood of our Lord Jesus Christ, the true vine."

Prayer of Thanksgiving

F

Many churches have covenants and/or creeds which can be a very special part of the Communion celebration. The reception of new members can also be a part of a Communion service. New members are appropriately received during the service and served their Communion, perhaps by the pastor.

Sermon or Communion Meditation

Invitation (*to be said by the minister before coming to the table*)

Reading of Names of Candidates for Membership

Communion Hymn (*New member candidates will come forward and take seats on the front row.*)

Reading of Church Covenant or Creed (*Samples are found in chapter 5.*)

Words of Institution

Prayer of Thanks

The Giving of the Bread

(The minister will pass the bread to the servers and will repeat the Words of Institution for the bread. Distribution is made to the people; and after the people are served, the minister will direct participation.)

Silent Prayer

The Giving of the Cup

(Same procedure as for the bread.)

Silent Prayer

Memorial Service

(This includes the reading of the names of the

members who have died since the last Commu-
nion, the reading of Revelation 14:13, and a
prayer of gratitude for the lives of the deceased
and for the bereaved.)
Offering for the Needy

G

The following service includes a responsive reading
as the invitation to the observance. It is not outlined in
detail, allowing for innovations.

Communion Hymn (*People sing softly or the choir*
sings as the bread and cup are later distributed.)
Words of Invitation and Response
MINISTER: I heard the voice of Jesus say,
      "Come unto Me and rest;
      Lay down, thou weary one, lay down
      Thy head upon My breast":

PEOPLE: I came to Jesus as I was,
      Weary, and worn, and sad;
      I found in Him a resting-place,
      And He has made me glad.

MINISTER: I heard the voice of Jesus say,
      "Behold, I freely give
      The living water; thirsty one,
      Stoop down, and drink, and live":

PEOPLE: I came to Jesus and I drank
      Of that life-giving stream;
      My thirst was quenched, my soul re-
vived,

And now I live in Him.

MINISTER: I heard the voice of Jesus say,
              "I am this dark world's light;
              Look unto Me, thy morn shall rise,
              And all thy day be bright":

PEOPLE: I looked to Jesus, and I found
              In Him my star, my sun;
              And in that light of life I'll walk
              Till travelling days are done.[3]

Prayer of Consecration
The Bread:
    Prayer   Serving   Participation
The Cup:
    Prayer   Serving   Participation
Prayer of Dedication
Benediction Hymn

H

In this final service the emphasis is upon reflection
and silent participation. The people are asked to read or
pray silently and then quietly receive and consume the
elements.

Service of the Lord's Supper

Words of Institution
    Jesus says: "Behold, I stand at the door, and
    knock: if any man hear my voice, and open the
    door, I will come in to him, and will sup with

him, and he with me'' (Revelation 3:20).

We say: ''Even so, come, Lord Jesus!'' (Revelation 22:20). And be thou to us both the Master of the Feast and Bread of Life.

Prayer of Dedication

''Almighty and most merciful Father; We have erred, and strayed from thy ways like lost sheep. We have followed too much the devices and desires of our own hearts. We have offended against thy holy laws. We have left undone those things which we ought to have done; And we have done those things which we ought not to have done; And there is no health in us. But thou, O Lord, have mercy upon us, miserable offenders. Spare thou those, O God, who confess their faults. Restore thou those who are penitent; According to thy promises declared unto mankind In Christ Jesus our Lord. And grant, O most merciful Father, for his sake; That we may hereafter live a godly, righteous, and sober life, To the glory of thy holy Name. Amen.''[4]

In silence the Bread and the Cup will be distributed without direction. You will receive the elements and consume them as you prepare your own heart.

Hymn

SPECIAL COMMUNION TIMES

The observance of the Lord's Supper can make special times in people's lives unforgettable. There are the traditional times when the service is appropriate, such as Holy Thursday, Christmas, and New Year's Eve. But the service can also make times such as retreats, small group get-togethers, and Sunday evening services special.

Instructions for special Communion services should be clearly understood for the participants to gain the most.

Advent Communion Service

Organ Prelude

Opening Sentence: "And he sent Peter and John, saying, Go and prepare us the passover, that we may eat" (Luke 22:8).

Hymn

Invocation (*unison*)

Come, O Lord, and dwell within our hearts this day. May our worship be acceptable in your sight as we proclaim through symbols the good news of the Messiah, even Jesus Christ, our Lord, in whose name we pray. Amen.

Welcome

Worship by sharing
Gospel Lesson
Hymn
Sermon
Hymn
Service of the Lord's Supper
    Words of Invitation
    Hymn of Communion
    Words of Institution
        We thank you, Father, that in the fullness of time
        you sent your Son to be Emmanuel, God with
        us. He came among us as a servant and a friend
        of sinners, and when he was despised and re-
        jected, he humbled himself in obedience to your
        will and freely accepted death on a cross. Father,
        send your Spirit on us and on these gifts of bread
        and the cup that in this holy sharing we may
        know the presence of the Christ, who gave his
        body and blood for us all.
    Sharing the Bread
        MINISTER: "As the loaf is one, so are we one
                     body. We share in the body of Christ,
                     with gratitude."
Prayer   *Distribution   Participation
Sharing the Cup
        MINISTER: "We take this cup, sharing Christ's
                     life and blood."

---

    *Congregation sings the song "Let Us Break Bread Together" softly
until distribution takes place: Repeat refrain throughout distribution.

Prayer   **Distribution   Participation
Hymn
Benediction

Advent Communion Service

Opening Sentence

"And he sent Peter and John, saying, Go and prepare us the passover, that we may eat" (Luke 22:8).

Hymn of Convocation

Invocation (*unison*)

Come, O Lord, and dwell within our hearts this night. May our worship be acceptable in thy sight as we proclaim through symbols the good news of the Messiah, even Jesus Christ our Lord, in whose name we pray. Amen.

Instruction Through the Scriptures

Ye Are My Disciples	John 13:1-20
The Bread of Life	John 6:25-35
The New Covenant	Matthew 26:26-46

Prayer

Invitation to the Lord's Supper

"Let Us Break Bread Together"

Choir and/or Congregation

*The Observance of Holy Communion

The Bread:

Preparation   Presentation   Participation

**The congregation sings "Let us drink the cup together on our knees." Repeat the refrain throughout distribution.

*Please retain the bread and the cup until all have been served, at which time the presiding person will instruct all to partake together.

The Cup:
    Preparation
                    Presentation
                                    Participation

Prayer of Thanksgiving
Hymn of Consecration
Silent Prayer and Benediction

A Silent Christmas Eve Communion

(All the following should be printed on programs.)

May the few minutes you spend here in God's house this evening be a time and a place of calm, peace, and quiet. Gather your thoughts and feelings unto yourself and permit the Spirit of Christ to permeate your total being. "For unto us a child is born, unto us a son is given: and the government shall be upon his shoulder: and his name shall be called Wonderful, Counseller, The mighty God, The everlasting Father, the Prince of Peace" (Isaiah 9:6).

Observe This Suggested Order of Worship

As you enter, be silent in the beauty of the sanctuary.
Take your seat and reflect over your past trials, blessings:
    make confession for neglected opportunities, sins,
        failures;
    surrender your negative, critical thoughts and doubts;
    reach out to others in prayer, to loved ones, to those
        in need, name those for whom you pray;
    pray for the church, the nation, and the world.
Read appropriate Scripture from pew Bibles or hymnals.
Project your thoughts to Bethlehem; consider what was

in the mind of God in the sending of Jesus.

Pray for the Presence of God.

Go forward to the chancel; kneel in prayer. When you
    are ready to receive the Communion elements, a
    server will serve you as you lift your head.

Return to your seat when you have been served; read a
    joyful carol of celebration.

Before you depart, prayerfully rededicate yourself to
    God and his will for your life and then depart in
    silent rejoicing.

A Christmas Service

Prelude

Greeting

> WORSHIP LEADER: ". . . behold, I bring you good
> tidings of great joy, which shall
> be to all people. For unto you
> is born this day . . . a Saviour,
> which is Christ the Lord" (Luke
> 2:10-11).

> PEOPLE: "Glory to God in the highest, and on earth
> peace, good will toward [his people]"
> (Luke 2:14).

Carol

Prayer

First Lesson: Luke 2:8-20

Carol

Second Lesson: Matthew 2:1-12

Gospel Lesson: John 3:16-17

Meditation

Response
>   Offering
>   Prayer
>   Hymn

Sharing the Bread and the Cup
>   The minister takes the bread and breaking it says,
>   "As the loaf is one, so are we one body. We share
>   in the body of Christ." Servers will distribute the
>   bread and the minister will declare when all have
>   been served, "We eat this bread in remembrance
>   of Him."
>
>   The minister takes the cup, saying: "We take this
>   cup sharing Christ's life and blood." When all have
>   been served, the minister will say, "The blood of
>   Christ is given for you," and lead in consuming the
>   cup.
>
>   When all have been served, have partaken, and are
>   waiting, the minister says, "The body of Christ is
>   given for you."
>
>   THE PEOPLE: Amen.

Carol: "Joy to the World"
Benediction

Maundy Thursday
His Friends and Enemies

Announcement: Matthew 26:1-2
Hymn
Invocation
Anointing of Jesus: Mark 14:3-9
Judas Plans Betrayal: Matthew 26:14-16

The Passover
Washing the Feet: John 13:1-16
Hymn
Designating Judas: Matthew 26:21-25
The Helper: John 16:4-7
The Lord's Supper: Mark 14:22-25

In Gethsemane
Jesus' Prayer: Mark 14:32-42
The Arrest: Mark 14:43-53

The Trials
Before Priests: Mark 14:54-65
Death of Judas: Matthew 27:3-10
Before Pilate: Mark 15:1-5
Request for Barabbas: Luke 23:18-23
Condemned: Matthew 27:24-31
Hymn

The Crucifixion
Simon of Cyrene: Luke 23:26
Hymn
Execution: Mark 15:22-32
The Malefactor: Luke 23:40-43
His Death: Matthew 27:45-54
His Burial: Mark 15:42-46
The Watch: Matthew 27:66
Hymn
Invitation
Words of Institution

Pre-Communion Prayer
The Bread
The Cup
Post-Communion Prayer
Hymn
Benediction[1]

Maundy Thursday Communion Service (1)

Preparation Moments
Call to Worship
Invocation
Hymn
Scripture Reading
Call to Confession

> "Come now, and let us reason together, saith the
> LORD: though your sins be as scarlet, they shall be
> as white as snow . . . " (Isaiah 1:18).

Prayer of Confession (*unison*)

> Heavenly Father, we turn to you in confession of
> our faithlessness. We have not always followed
> your way. We do not live as we know we ought to
> live. We have not always heeded your voice. We
> have stopped our ears and hardened our hearts and
> have often turned away from your kingdom. But
> we desire to begin a new life. We want to shake
> off the strong bonds of sin and faithlessness. We
> pray that you will forgive us. Make new our love
> for you, your church, and our brothers. Renew our
> zeal to follow your commandments, and help us to
> live faithful, thankful, and joyful lives. Amen.

Words of Assurance
Hymn
Meditation
Prayer of Access and Consecration (*unison*)

> Almighty God, who by the gift of Jesus Christ opened for us a new and better way of life, cleanse the thoughts of our hearts, blot out our faithlessness, that drawing near to you with humble hearts we may receive these gifts of bread and wine for our strength and your glory. We pray that your presence will now bless and make sacred these common elements so that, as they become one with us, we may become one with you. In the name and spirit of Jesus Christ. Amen.

Invitation
Words of Institution
Distribution and Participation in Silence
Silent Prayer
Prayer of Thanksgiving
Invitation to Christian Discipleship
Hymn
Benediction and Organ Postlude

Maundy Thursday Communion Service (2)

This is a special service to commemorate the first Lord's Supper. It is a service in which we seek communion with the living Lord. You are urged to sacrifice whatever ill feelings you may harbor in your heart in order that you may experience his presence. Rid yourself of all resentment, hate, pride, or suspicion. Bring your-

self to humility of heart where you may truly confess
and seek forgiveness. Thus, you may receive the bread
and the cup and have your stature increased in God's
sight.

Invitation and Call to Worship

Hymn

Prayer (*in unison*)

> Almighty God, whose blessed Son Jesus Christ did
> ordain the holy meal as a memorial of his death and
> the communion of his risen life, grant that we may
> approach his table with love and humble hope, that
> we may be united with him and with each other by
> the power of his love. Through Jesus Christ our
> Lord. Amen.

Scripture: Luke 22:7-23

Doxology

Prayer for Purity (*in unison*)

> "Almighty God, unto whom all hearts are open,
> all desires known, and from whom no secrets are
> hid; Cleanse the thoughts of our hearts by the in-
> spiration of thy Holy Spirit, that we may perfectly
> love thee, and worthily magnify thy holy Name;
> through Christ our Lord. Amen."[2]

Examination of Conscience Response

> MINISTER: Hear what our Lord Jesus Christ saith:
> "The first of all the commandments is,
> Hear, O Israel; The Lord our God is one
> Lord: And thou shalt love the Lord thy
> God with all thy heart, and with all thy
> soul, and with all thy mind, and with

all thy strength: this is the first commandment. And the second is like,
namely this, Thou shalt love thy neigh-
bor as thyself. There is none other commandment greater than these'' (Mark
12:29-31).

PEOPLE: Lord, have mercy upon us, and write all
these your laws in our hearts, we beseech
you.

MINISTER: ''A new commandment I give unto you,
That ye love one another; as I have
loved you, that ye also love one another'' (John 13:34).

PEOPLE: Lord, have mercy upon us, and write all
these your laws in our hearts, we beseech
you.

Prayer of Confession (*in unison*)

''Almighty God, Father of our Lord Jesus Christ,
Maker of all things, Judge of all men; We acknowledge and bewail our manifold sins and wickedness,
Which we, from time to time, most grievously have
committed, By thought, word, and deed, Against
thy Divine Majesty, Provoking most justly thy
wrath and indignation against us. We do earnestly
repent, And are heartily sorry for these our mis-
doings; The remembrance of them is grievous unto
us; The burden of them is intolerable. Have mercy
upon us, Have mercy upon us, most merciful Father;
For thy Son our Lord Jesus Christ's sake, Forgive
us all that is past; And grant that we may ever

hereafter Serve and please thee In newness of life,
To the honour and glory of thy Name; Through
Jesus Christ our Lord. Amen.''[3]

Absolution *(pastor)*

> May the almighty and merciful Lord grant unto you
> pardon, absolution, and remission of all your sins,
> time for amendment of life, and the comfort of his
> Holy Spirit. Amen.

Extinguishing of Lenten Candles

> We put out this Lenten Candle remembering:
>
> 1. how Peter tempted Jesus to stay away from
>   Jerusalem. (Matthew 16:21-23)
> 2. how Judas sought to betray Jesus. (Matthew
>   26:14-16)
> 3. how Peter, James, and John slept when Jesus
>   asked them to watch and pray. (Matthew
>   26:36-46)
> 4. how Peter three times denied that he ever
>   knew Jesus. (Matthew 26:69-75)
> 5. how all the disciples forsook Jesus and fled.
>   (Matthew 26:52-56)
> 6. how the crowd shouted, ''Crucify him! Cru-
>   cify him!'' (Matthew 27:15-23)
> 7. how all of us by our sins have denied and
>   betrayed Jesus. (Matthew 27:32-44)

Service of Communion

> Words of Institution
>
> Consecration, Fraction, Distribution
>
> *(Let each person break off a piece of the bread
> and hold it until told to eat.)*

The Cup, Poured Out, Distribution
(After words of consecration, each will hold his or her cup until instructed to drink.)
Prayer of Thanksgiving (*in unison*)
Almighty and everliving God, we thank you for feeding us at your table. May this bread and cup sustain us in obedience to Jesus Christ our Lord. Grant to us a sure vision of your purpose for the world, a share of your love for us, and a faith that will not be daunted by difficulty or lack of response. Consecrate the labors of this day, that in this congregation the Word may be faithfully preached and we may continue in a goodly fellowship of your faithful people. Through Jesus Christ our Lord. Amen.

Hymn
Greet One Another

A Maundy Thursday Candlelight Communion

At this service lay leaders have the principal parts in the program. The pulpit and other settings are removed from the rostrum, and a long table is placed in the center, at the ends of which and along the back side deacons or other participants are seated on either side of the pastor. On the table are placed the elements of Communion and the following order of service is followed:[4]

The Vigil of Maundy Thursday

We are commemorating the Passion of the Lord from the hour of fellowship in the upper room to the hour of loneliness in the Garden of Gethsemane.

Hymn

Call to Worship: Psalm 27:1-4

READER I: Your word, O Lord, has bidden us to behold your beauty and to inquire in your temple. Therefore, have we come as inquiring children.

Creation

Scripture: Genesis 1:1-5

Choir: First stanza of a Communion hymn

READER II: We light a candle at the remembrance of the creation of the world and our own creation (*lights candle on the table*). I believe that God has created me and all that exists; that he has given to me and still preserves my body and soul with all my limbs and senses, my reason and all the faculties of my mind, together with my raiment, food, home, and family, and all my property; that he daily provides me abundantly with all the necessities of life, protects me from all danger, and preserves me and guards me against all evil; all of which he does out of pure paternal and divine goodness and mercy, without any merit or worthiness in me; for all of which I am in duty bound to thank, praise, serve, and obey him. This is most certainly true.

Redemption

Scripture: John 1:1-13

Choir: Second stanza of a Communion hymn

READER III: We in thankful devotion light a candle reminding us that in Jesus Christ we have redemption (*lights second candle*). I believe that Jesus

Christ is true God, begotten of the Father from eternity, and also true man, born of the Virgin Mary. He is my Lord, who has redeemed me, a lost and condemned creature, secured and delivered me from all sins, from death and from the power of the devil, not with silver and gold, but with his holy and precious blood, and with his innocent sufferings and death, in order that I might be his, live under him in his kingdom, and serve him in everlasting righteousness, innocence, and blessedness, even as he is risen from the dead, and lives and reigns through all eternity. This is most certainly true.

Obedience

Scripture: Acts 2:1-4

Choir: Third stanza of a Communion hymn

READER IV: We light a third candle reminding us, O God, that you appeared as a pillar of fire by day to lead your people through the wilderness; you visited the hillside in a flaming bush to call your servant; and you came in the fullness of your Spirit on the day of Pentecost. Now you visit our hearts, purifying them and making us meet to be called your children (*lights third candle*). I believe that I cannot by my own reason or strength believe, trust, and serve Jesus Christ, my Lord; but the Holy Spirit through the Scriptures enlightens me, sanctifies and preserves me in true faith, and directs my life to be one of usefulness to him. He, I believe, forgives all my sins and the sins of all believers, and will raise me and all the dead at the last day, and will grant everlasting life to me and to all who believe and trust in him. Jesus Christ died for our redemption. He arose again victorious over sin and death. Through him we are victors also. This is most certainly true.

Choir: Fourth Stanza of a Communion hymn

Scripture: Matthew 5:14-16

Choir: Hums a hymn as choir members proceed to the table and light individual candles from the three burning on the table and then they light the candles of the worshipers in the congregation.

Prayer of Thanksgiving for the Bread and the Cup

The Bread:	Distribution	Participation
The Cup:	Distribution	Participation

Benediction

A Time of Fellowship

A Silent Communion Service for Evening Worship

Organ Prelude

Hymn: "Day Is Dying in the West"

Silent Prayer

Response by the Choir or Soloist (*one verse of a prayer hymn*)

Evening Hymn: "Jesus, the Very Thought of Thee"

Silent Prayer

Response by the Choir

Communion Hymn (*standing*)

Special Appropriate Music by Choir or Soloist

Service of the Bread

Special Music
Service of the Wine
Hymn
Silent Prayer
Response by the Choir
Silent Prayer
Benediction
Postlude

No words should be spoken. The service proceeds without any announcements. The elders or deacons are instructed beforehand so they will know what to do and when to do it. When it is time to pass the elements, the pastor simply elevates the bread and then the cup in silent blessing, then passes it to those serving, who distribute it while the organ plays softly.

Communion and Consecration Service

The following instructions should be printed on the program:

This service of Communion is designed to give you an opportunity to consecrate yourself to Christ and his kingdom's interest. The circumstances of the table and candles and bread and cup are used to bring us nearer to the actual circumstances of the first Lord's Supper. The service can be meaningful only to you who will sincerely repent and honestly consecrate yourselves. At the conclusion of the service please refrain from talk and depart quietly with God's blessing.

Words of Invitation
Prayer

MINISTER: Let us pray. Almighty God, whose blessed Son Jesus Christ did ordain the holy sacrament as a memorial of his death and the communion of his risen life, grant that we may approach his table with love and humble hope; that we may be united with him and with our brothers and sisters by the power of his love. Through Jesus Christ our Lord.

PEOPLE: Amen.

Scripture Reading: Luke 22:7-20

Doxology

Meditation

Service of Holy Communion

Prayer of Confession (*in unison*)

O Lord, forgive us, for we know we have failed you in many ways and have made many mistakes. Like the disciples of old we have often forsaken your Son and fled from his presence. Forgive us, we pray. Free us from the power of sin and enable us to live according to your holy ways, through Jesus Christ our Lord. Amen.

Absolution

May the almighty and merciful Lord grant unto you pardon, absolution, and remission of all your sins, time for amendment of life, and the comfort of his Holy Spirit. Amen.

Offertory (*in unison*)

Here, O Lord, we offer and present unto you, ourselves, our souls and bodies, to be a reasonable, holy, and living sacrifice; humbly beseeching you that you will accept this our offering, and use it for the work of your kingdom, and the making known of your love to all people, through Jesus Christ our Lord.

Words of Institution

Consecration, Fraction, and Distribution

(Let each person break off a piece of the bread as it is passed and hold it until all eat together. The cup is a common cup. Each one will take a sip and pass the cup to the next person when instructed.)

Prayer of Thanksgiving *(in unison)*

Almighty and everliving God, we most heartily thank you for feeding us at your table. May this bread and cup sustain us in obedience to Jesus Christ our Lord. Grant to us a sure vision of your purpose for the world, a share of your love for all people, and a faith that will not be daunted by difficulty or lack of response. Consecrate the labors of this day that in this congregation the Word may be faithfully preached and we may continue in a goodly fellowship of your faithful people. Through Jesus Christ our Lord.

Hymn: "Blest Be the Tie that Binds"

Worldwide Communion

Organ Prelude

The Choral Call to Worship

Hymn

The Invocation and the Lord's Prayer

The Welcome and Registration
The Prayer of Dedication
The Presentation of Tithes and Offerings
The Reading of Holy Scripture
An Anthem
The Communion Meditation
The Invitation Hymn
The Introduction and Invitation to the Communion
The Communion Hymm
The Words of Institution (*in unison*)

"Come unto me, all ye that labour and are heavy laden, and I will give you rest" (Matthew 11:28). "As the heart panteth after the water brooks, so panteth my soul after thee, O God" (Psalm 42:1). "Blessed are they which do hunger and thirst after righteousness: for they shall be filled" (Matthew 5:6). "My soul thirsteth for God, for the living God . . ." (Psalm 42:2).

The Bread:
  Prayer   Distribution   Participation
The Cup:
  Prayer   Distribution   Participation
The Prayer of Dedication *(Minister and People)*

Almighty God, our Father, pour out your spirit upon us that we may have new vision, new life, and new fellowship with you. Open our hearts that we may see Christ with hands outstretched to bless. Do with us what you will and as you will. Hasten the day when the whole earth shall be filled with the knowledge of you and when everyone shall

dwell together as brothers and sisters, through Jesus
Christ our Lord. Amen.
The World Mission Offering
The Benediction
The Choral Response
The Organ Response

Special (Small Group) Communion Service

This service is suitable for a small group, seated in
a circle, perhaps in a room not a sanctuary.

The Preparation
Introduction
   The pastor or leader explains that the congregation
   is assembled in the name of Christ and instructs
   them to pray for the Spirit.
Silence and Personal Confessions
   If desired, people may speak aloud of their failures,
   problems, etc.
Intercession
   People will write names of their family and anyone
   they are concerned for on a slip of paper. The slips
   will be passed to the person in charge. He or she
   will say, "Bless, O Lord, your servant _____
   and his loved ones. _____ ."
   The congregation will respond, "Bless, O Lord,
   your servants and keep them forever" after each set
   of names.
Thanksgiving
   Everyone is invited to stand and express gratitude

to God and to others for whom they are especially thankful.

The Communion
Passing the Bread

> The presider will take the plate with the loaf on it, break the bread, and pass the plate saying, "The gift of God for the people of God." The receiver will receive the plate and respond, "Amen." Each person will then pass the plate, breaking off a portion of the bread to consume later when instructed and will repeat the words of the presider to the next person. When the plate returns to the presider, he or she will take the plate, elevate it, and say, "The body of the Lord Jesus Christ, the Bread of Life." At this time all persons consume their bread simultaneously.

The Cup

> The cup (*one cup*) is done the same way, with the words "The blood of our Lord Jesus Christ, the true vine."

After all have been served, a prayer of thanks will be given by the leader. A hymn without accompaniment is sung from memory.

The Dismissal
LEADER: "Go and serve the Lord. You are free."
Celebration: Share love and appreciation.

Communion with the Sick
Opening Words

"God shows his love for us in that while we were
yet sinners Christ died for us." (Romans 5:8, RSV).

Invocation

"Almighty God, unto whom all hearts are open,
all desires known, and from whom no secrets are
hid; Cleanse the thoughts of our hearts by the inspiration of thy Holy Spirit, that we may perfectly
love thee, and worthily magnify thy holy Name;
through Christ our Lord. Amen."[5]

Scripture Reading: Psalm 23

A Brief Meditation or Thoughts Shared

Prayer of Thanks for the Bread and Cup

Words of Institution for the Bread

"As they were eating, he took bread, and blessed,
and broke it, and gave it to them, and said, 'Take;
this is my body!'" (Mark 14:22, RSV)

Words of Institution for the Cup

"And he took a cup, and when he had given thanks
he gave it to them, and they all drank of it. And
he said to them, 'This is my blood of the covenant,
which is poured out for many'" (Mark 14:23-24,
RSV).

The Lord's Prayer in Unison

Benediction

Communion Breakfast (1)

A breakfast can be a great opportunity for Communion; the eating of the meal may be part of the service.
A Lenten or Advent breakfast is most appropriate. Put
rolls and juice on the tables with the breakfast items.

Hymn or Carol
Breaking the Bread (*The leader will give the words for the bread and break the roll and ask the attenders to do likewise, or the leader may pass his or her roll to others.*)
Prayer of Thanksgiving for the Bread and the Meal
Eating, Sharing with each other
After the Meal
    Hymn or Carol
        Scripture: Perhaps each would like to recite a favorite verse.
        Concerns: People are allowed to share with the group any concerns or blessings they wish.
Hymn
Prayer: Everyone is invited to offer short prayers during this period.
Scripture: Matthew's account of the Supper
Sharing the Cup
The Lord's Prayer
Dismissal

A Communion Breakfast (2)

The people enter the dining room and take their seats at the tables in silence. An outline of consideration for prayer is provided at each plate.

Quiet Moments (*As music is played very quietly, all meditate and pray for approximately three minutes.*)
Hymn
Scripture: Luke 18:9-14   Lay Leader

Meditation (*five minutes or so*)	Pastor
Communion Hymn	
Invitation	Pastor
Prayer of Confession	Lay Leader
Assurance of Forgiveness	Pastor
Words of Institution	Pastor
Distribution	

> *(Participants will break a piece of bread from the loaf at each table, pass the loaf, and hold the bread until the pastor directs to eat. There should be a chalice or cup at each table. The pastor will instruct to drink, and each will sip and pass.)*

Prayer
The Lord's Prayer (*in unison*)
Benediction
Breakfast Together in Fellowship

Communion at the Wedding Service

Many young people wish to incorporate the Communion service into the marriage ceremony. The following order can be used. After the couple have been pronounced man and wife, the minister says: "As a further act of consecration, please approach the Communion table, where you have the opportunity to consecrate yourselves and your marriage to Christ and his kingdom's interest."

Prayer: Almighty God, grant that this couple may approach Christ's table with love and humble hope; grant that they may be united with him by the power of his love. Enable them to live according to your holy ways through Jesus Christ, our Lord and Savior. Amen.

The couple will kneel and after a moment of silent praying, the minister will serve them.

The couple will then rise, face the congregation, and the minister will introduce them: ''Ladies and gentlemen, may I present to you Mr. & Mrs. _____.''

Congregational participation in Communion is also appropriate and ushers may be enlisted to serve guests who would join the families in the observance. This procedure should be evaluated by each church according to its accepted practices.

COMMUNION SERVICES
WITH THEMES

Following are worship services utilizing a single theme and incorporating the Lord's Supper. The sermon as such is split into sections, but a basic unity is easy to maintain with the portions of the service supporting the central theme. Examples using several themes are included. Other themes which might be included are the last week of Christ on earth, the resurrection, hope, New Year, Pentecost, love, etc.

Communion Symbols

Organ Prelude
Church Concerns
Call to Worship
Hymn
Prayer
Introduction of the Theme

The Bread
Scripture: Mark 14:1, 18, 22
Exposition
Pastoral Prayer

The Cup
Scripture: Luke 22:17-20
Exposition

The Lord's Supper: The Bread   The Cup
Choral Offering

The Towel
Scripture: John 13:3-16
Exposition
Hymn
Offering
Hymn
Hand of Fellowship
Benediction
Organ Postlude

The Prayer of John 17
Organ Prelude
Call to Worship
Hymn
Invocation

I. Christ Prays for Himself
The Scripture: John 17:1-5
Exposition of the Scripture
Silent Prayer   Morning Prayer   Response

II. Christ Prays for His Disciples
The Scripture: John 17:6-12
Exposition of the Scriptures
Requests for Prayer of Members
Silent Prayer
Choral Selection

III. Christ Prays for His Mission
The Scripture: John 17:13-19
Exposition of the Scripture
Hymn

IV. Christ Prays for the World
The Scripture: John 17:20-26
Worship of Sharing
Offertory

V. Answering Christ's Prayer
Reading of Statement of Faith or Covenant
Observance of the Lord's Supper
    The Bread and the Cup
    The Communion Offering for the Needy
    Communion Hymn
The Benediction
Organ Postlude

Themes of the Lord's Supper
Organ Prelude
Choral Call to Worship
Call to Worship Response (*in unison*)
    "Who shall ascend into the hill of the LORD? or
who shall stand in his holy place? He that hath
clean hands, and a pure heart; who hath not lifted
up his soul unto vanity, nor sworn deceitfully. He
shall receive the blessing from the LORD, and righteousness from the God of his salvation" (Psalm
24:3-5).
Hymn

Invocation and the Lord's Prayer (*in unison*)

"Lord, thou hast been our dwelling place in all generations. . . . O satisfy us early with thy mercy; that we may rejoice and be glad all our days. Make us glad according to the days wherein thou hast afflicted us, and the years wherein we have seen evil. Let thy work appear unto thy servants, and thy glory unto their children. And let the beauty of the LORD our God be upon us: and establish thou the work of our hands upon us; yea, the work of our hands establish thou it" (Psalm 90:1, 14-17).

Comfort
Scripture: John 6:31-37
Exposition of Theme
Pastoral Prayer

Remembrance
Scripture: I Corinthians 11:23-25
Exposition of Theme
Anthem

The Supper
Observance of the Lord's Supper
    Hymn
    Words of Institution
      The Bread   The Cup
    Prayer   Distribution   Participation

Fellowship
Scripture: 1 John 1:5-7
Exposition of Theme

Hymn
Offering

Anticipation
Scripture: 1 Corinthians 11:26
Exposition of Theme
Invitation Hymn
Benediction
Response
Organ Postlude

The Trinity

I. Introduction
Prelude
Choral Call to Worship
Hymn
Gloria Patri
Introduction of the Theme

II. God, the Father
Psalm 103:13; Matthew 6:9; Galatians 4:6
Welcome
  Registration
  Reminders
Worship of Sharing:
  Doxology
  Prayer
  Offerings
Anthem

III. God, the Son
John 20:26-29; Colossians 2:9; 2 Corinthians 4:6

Exposition of the Theme
Youth Ensemble
The Lord's Supper
    Communion Hymn
    Words of Invitation
    The Bread:
        Prayer   Distribution   Participation
    The Cup:
        Prayer   Distribution   Participation

IV. God, the Holy Spirit
Luke 11:13; Romans 8:26-27
Exposition of the Theme

V. The Conclusion
2 Corinthians 13:14
Exposition of the Theme
Invitation Hymn

Benediction
Choral Response
Organ Postlude

The Church

Prelude
Choral Call to Worship
Introduction of the Theme
Hymn
Invocation
Lord's Prayer
I. The Church: What Is It?
Text: 1 Peter 2:9-10
Exposition of the Theme

Announcements and Registration
Worship of Sharing:
Doxology
Prayer
Tithes and Offerings
Anthem
II. The Church: Body of Christ
Text: Ephesians 5:29-30
Exposition of the Theme
Youth Choir
The Lord's Supper
Words of Institution
Communion Hymn
The Bread:
Prayer   Distribution   Participation
The Cup:
Prayer   Distribution   Participation
III. The Church: Militant
Text: Matthew 16:18
Exposition of the Theme
Invitation Hymn
Benediction
Organ Postlude

The Church

Organ Prelude
Choral Call to Worship
Hymn
Invocation
The Lord's Prayer

The Church of Jesus
Scripture: Luke 4:16-32
Anthem
Pastoral Prayer
The Church at Philippi
Scripture: Philippians 1:1-11
Exposition
The Church's Fellowship
Welcome and Registration
Sharing in Worship
Fellowship at the Lord's Table
    Communion Hymn
    The Bread:
        Prayer   Distribution   Participation
    The Cup:
        Prayer   Distribution   Participation

The Church Growing
Invitation Hymn
Benediction
Organ Postlude

Stewardship
Organ Prelude
Call to Worship
Hymn
Invocation and the Lord's Prayer
Of Possessions
Scripture: Matthew 19:16-22
Exposition
Worship of Sharing

Of Abilities
Scripture: 1 Corinthians 12:4-11
Exposition
Anthem
Of Time
Scripture: Mark 13:32-35
Exposition
Of Life
Scripture: James 4:13-17
Exposition
Hymn
Service of the Lord's Supper
    Words of Invitation
    Communion Hymn (*verses 1 and 2*)
    The Bread
      Institution,   Prayer,   Participation
    The Cup
      Institution,   Prayer,   Participation
Hymn (*verses 3 and 4*)
Benediction and Organ Postlude

Christmas and Communion
The Holy Family
Prelude
Choral Call to Worship: "O Come, O Come,
  Emmanuel"
Introduction of the Theme
Hymn
Invocation
The Lord's Prayer

I. The Holy Family: Joseph
Text: Matthew 1:1, 16
Exposition of the Theme
Announcements and Registration
Doxology
Prayer of Dedication
Presentation of Tithes and Offerings
Anthem

II. The Holy Family: Mary
Text: Luke 1:26-31
Exposition of the Theme
Silent Prayer and Meditation
Morning Prayer
Choral Response

III. The Holy Family: Jesus
Text: Matthew 1:18-21
Exposition of the Theme
Invitation Hymn
The Lord's Supper
    Invitation and Words of Institution
    Communion Hymn
    The Bread:
      Prayer   Distribution   Participation
    The Cup:
      Prayer   Distribution   Participation
Hymn
Benediction
Choral Response
Organ Postlude

SERVICE RESOURCES

I n this chapter of service resources examples of the following kinds of resources are included: words of invitation, words of institution, pre-Communion prayers, post-Communion prayers, words of participation, words of conclusion, creeds, and statements.

Words of Invitation

For the participants to enter fully into the drama portrayed around the Lord's table, the words of invitation are very important.

The invitation establishes the basis for participation in the Communion. In these words the minister can call everyone to repentance of sin, to loving acceptance of one another, and to obedience to God. Emphasis on the penitential character is essential, but the celebration of the privilege to participate should not be neglected.

Seasonal observances can be incorporated into these words and the words of institution.

• • •

Christian, approach this observance in penitence, and Christ will meet you in mercy. Enter with your human vows, and God will meet you with his promises. Come, hungry and thirsty, and be fed with the nourishing bread and cup.

• • •

"Behold, I stand at the door, and knock, if any man hear my voice, and open the door, I will come in to him, and will sup with him, and he with me" (Revelation 3:20). ". . . he that cometh to me shall never hunger; and he that believeth on me shall never thirst" (John 6:35).

• • •

"We are now about to observe the ordinance of the Lord's Supper. This table of the Lord is open to all fellow Christians; and although none should partake of these sacred emblems impenitent or without faith in Christ, we cordially invite all who are sincerely seeking him to come to his table, in the assurance that he who came into the world to be the Saviour of all will in no wise cast them out.

"Come to this sacred table, not because you must, but because you may; come to testify not that you are righteous, but that you sincerely love our Lord Jesus Christ, and desire to be his true disciples; come, not because you are strong, but because you are weak; not because you have any claim on heaven's rewards, but because in your frailty and sin you stand in constant need of heaven's mercy and help; come, not to express an opinion, but to seek a Presence and pray for a Spirit."[1]

• • •

Let us come to this table not trusting in our own righteousness but in the mercy of our Lord. Here we are to offer and present to him, ourselves, our souls and our bodies. Everyone who takes of the bread and the cup pledges oneself to share God's love with others. Let us draw near to partake of the symbols of his broken body and his shed blood.

• • •

We remember how Jesus the Risen Lord was known to his friends in the breaking of bread; their hearts were set ablaze as they talked with him on the road to Damascus. We pray that the Lord Jesus will make himself known to us in the breaking of bread and that we will go from this place with hearts aflame with love. Let us tell God of our sins and depend on him in his goodness to forgive us.

• • •

Our God is trying to speak to us in the common things and in the common experiences of life; and in the midst of time he seeks to give us glimpses of eternity. May his Spirit come to us through this bread and this cup. May the Spirit tell us of Christ's sacrifice, confront us with his love, and fill us with his life.

• • •

Come to this table not because you are strong but because you are weak. Come, not because any goodness of your own gives you a right to come, but because you need mercy and help. Come because you love Christ and would like to love him more. Come because he loves you and gave himself for you. Let the bread and the cup be tokens and pledges of the grace of the Lord Jesus Christ, the love of God, and the fellowship of the Spirit.

• • •

Join others about the Table of the Lord with Christ as

our host. Receive forgiveness and reconciliation. For all
your broken promises to God, for your broken relation-
ships with others, let the bread and cup speak of peace
and pardon. Renew today your pledge of loyalty to Christ
and the kingdom.

• • •

We thank God for this Communion Day that unites us
with Christians of all races and lands. The love and
mercy of God are dramatically communicated by the
bread and the cup. You are invited to share his mercy
and love as we share these symbols.

• • •

Draw near with open heart and mind. Let the Spirit of
God give us a new vision, new life, and new fellowship.
Let us open our hearts that we may see Christ with hands
outstretched to bless us. May we go from here to hasten
the day when all persons shall dwell together as brothers
and sisters, through Jesus Christ as Lord.

• • •

If you sincerely turn from your sins and if you want to
live in love and peace with everyone, if you desire to
lead a new life doing God's will, then in faith receive
these elements. Let us make peace with God and be
confident of his forgiveness as we receive the bread and
the cup.

• • •

"Ye that do truly and earnestly repent of your sins, and
are in love and charity with your neighbors, and intend
to lead a new life, following the commandments of God
and walking from henceforth in his holy ways; draw near

with faith, and take this holy Sacrament to your comfort; and devoutly kneeling, make your humble confession to Almighty God.'' [2]

• • •

We are called to draw near in this Communion service. We seek God's grace through this ordinance. Let us have sincere sorrow for past sins and a willingness to confess unto God. We must seek mercy and forgiveness and dedicate ourselves earnestly to walk before the Lord in newness and holiness of life. It is thusly that we will receive present and everlasting comfort from this service.

• • •

We turn aside from our other activities and gather from many places in this place of worship. We come with contrite hearts and thoughtful minds and submissive wills. Through our love we become a true community. This table becomes a sacred place of thanksgiving and dedication. Let us partake unto the nourishment of our souls.

• • •

All who are disciples are invited to an upper room where Christ, the Lord, will minister to them. Here, let us be cleansed and made whole. Here, let the bread of life be broken to you and let the cup of blessing be poured out for you. This place now becomes for us the large upper room, for Christ is our host.

• • •

We are gathered together again in our spiritual home. Now we are invited to His table of grace. Now let our souls hunger for the things which He hast prepared for

them that love Him. Be not indifferent to His presence
nor listless to the gifts of His grace. May the glory of
the Lord be upon us as we eat this bread and drink this
cup.

• • •

We invite you now to receive the bread and the cup and
in so doing receive grace through our Lord Jesus Christ.
Turn from all pride or whatever needs his cleansing
touch. Realize that no secrets are hidden from him.
Rejoice that we have a Savior. Let praise, love, and
thanksgiving flow freely from your heart. Remember
that Christ died for you and ever liveth and abideth in
our midst.

• • •

In this hallowed service we are to lift our hearts unto
God. Our presence is our prayer, our need is our plea,
our assurance is God's faithfulness. Let us repent of all
that has made our lives so earthbound, darkened our
lives with guilt and shame, enslaved our wills, and made
us neglect our spiritual needs. We bless our Savior, Jesus
Christ, for being the Light that shines in our darkness
and for his precious grace and matchless love. Kneel
humbly and receive these sacred symbols.

• • •

"I come, not because I am worthy; not for any righteousness of mine; for I have grievously sinned and
fallen short of what, by God's help, I might have been.

"I come, not because there is any magic in partak-
ing of the symbols of Christ's body and blood.

"I come, not from a sense of duty that is unacquainted with deep appreciation for this blessed means of grace—the highest privilege in Christian worship.

"I come, because Christ bids me come. It is His table, and He extends the invitation.

"I come because it is a memorial to Him, as often as it is done in remembrance of Him. Here is vivid portrayal of the redeeming sacrifice of the Christ of Calvary. His matchless life, His victorious sufferings, and His faithfulness even unto death, are brought to mind, and I bow humbly before Him and worship.

"I come because in contemplation of the Father and His Son our Saviour, I am moved to thanksgiving for so great a salvation." [3]

• • •

Scriptures appropriate for Invitation follow:

John 6:51, 53-56;

John 4:14;   Revelation 22:17*b*;

Matthew 11:28-30;

Revelation 3:20;   John 15:1, 4, 5, 8

• • •

Worldwide Communion

A. You are invited to join with fellow believers throughout the world and believers down through the centuries who have found the light that never fades, a joy that no power can remove, forgiveness that is complete, and a love that is our assurance. We are mindful of the unseen cloud of witnesses who compass us about as well as the inspiration and prayers of the many believers of every land and nation.

B. "This do in remembrance of me." Thus, the Lord summons all his people.

> Come, with the comfort of his love;
> Come, with the sense of his grace;
> Come, with the knowledge of his wisdom;
> Come, with the assurance of his power;
> Come, with the joy of his presence;
> Come, with the hope of his promise.

Come with Christians all over the world on this Worldwide Communion Day. Perhaps we will be expressing our praise and adoration in a thousand tongues, but we participate in one faith. We will be in thousands of different places, but we will be one great fellowship. Let us abide in him and He in us. [4]

C. Today in many countries throughout the world the Communion service will unite Christians of all denominations in a spiritual fellowship that transcends all barriers. As we partake of these sacred elements, we do so in a universal emphasis upon personal commitment to Jesus Christ and rededication to his cause. Let us be resolved to apply the spiritual insights we gather from this service. Let us envision a new world, a world united, a world marked by Christian service to our neighbors.

● ● ●

Words of Institution

Some of the following words of institution are taken from Scripture. These words may be printed in the worship outline and be repeated in unison, read by the leader in their entirety, or arranged responsively.

These words are instructive for the people and help everyone gain an understanding of the meaning of Communion as an obedient act of worship.

Ours is a world broken. Signaling this brokenness are war, unrest, divorce, injustice, racism, poverty, sorrow. The world groans with its burdens. People's lives are cursed with hatreds, injustices, and disillusionments. Our broken world is a reflection of humankind's broken relationship with God. At this table today we are reminded that reconciliation is possible. The bread and the cup remind us that the breaks can be mended. To everyone of us who feels torn within, this supper speaks of wholeness.

• • •

"And as they were eating, [Jesus] took bread, and when he had blessed, he brake it, and gave to them, and said, Take ye: this is my body. And he took a cup and when he had given thanks, he gave to them: and they all drank of it. And he said unto them, This is my blood of the covenant, which is poured out for many. Verily I say unto you, I shall no more drink of the fruit of the vine, until that day when I drink it new in the kingdom of God.

"And when they had sung a hymn, they went out unto the Mount of Olives" (Mark 14:22-25, ASV).

• • •

These are the symbols of his blood and body. This

Communion is an acted parable. We take these symbols to commemorate his life and death. We express our faith that Christ is risen to be with us. We express our hope that we will be with him until the end of time. Let Jesus become a living reality now and always.

● ● ●

As you receive the bread and the cup, repent of your every sin known to you. Forsake your own goodness and trust him and his love for you. Christ has invited us to come. We come as his guests. May this memorial meal be a turning point in your life. Trust him and become secure.

● ● ●

We have been accustomed to thinking of the bread and the cup as the symbols of Christ in his weakness and death. Today let us think of them as symbols of the most dynamic power for good ever released to all humanity. The bread symbolizes the physical life of Jesus surrendered for us. The cup symbolizes the spiritual life supplied to us. The service portrays the power with which God saves us, the power of love and forgiveness.

● ● ●

When I survey the wondrous cross
On which the Prince of glory died,
My richest gain I count but loss,
And pour contempt on all my pride.

Forbid it, Lord, that I should boast,
Save in the death of Christ, my God;
All the vain things that charm me most
I sacrifice them to his blood.[5]

• • •

Beloved, this is the joyful feast of the people of God; come from the East and the West, and from the North and the South and gather about the table of the Lord. Behold, how good and pleasant it is when people dwell in unity. The peace of our Lord Jesus Christ be with us all.

• • •

Let us be led by Jesus Christ to draw near. We are beneath the shadow of his cross. We would meditate and pray. Remember that Christ has eaten with us the bread and drank the cup of our lives, and that he has had communion with us in our joy and sorrow, and tasted what it is for a man to die. Remember the beauty of his life, his obedience unto death, the charity of his cross, and his victory over the world's sin and sorrow. May our hearts be impressed and quickened with the memory of our Master and Savior.

• • •

Scriptures: Mark 14:22-25; Matthew 26:26-29; Luke 22:15-20; 1 Corinthians 11:23-24

• • •

Worldwide Communion

A. We do not at the table have our own private fellowship with the Host. We are there together, as children of God, in communion with one another and with Christ. The Lord's Supper becomes the great "family" meal of Christendom. We may have our separate altars, but all altars become one the world over as penitent believers sit or kneel or stand to receive the

Lord's Supper. It is not strange that Holy Communion has been held sacred by the children of God since that first night in the upper room. There, in the most intimate hour of his earthly fellowship with his own, Christ instituted the Supper for all his children for all the centuries. All Christians everywhere sense that in coming to their table or altar they are indeed coming to one great common place, the place where the Lord meets them with his indescribable mercy.

B. "'I am the living bread which came down from heaven; if any one eats of this bread, he will live for ever; and the bread which I shall give for the life of the world is my flesh.' . . . 'Truly, truly, I say to you, unless you eat the flesh of the Son of man and drink his blood, you have no life in you; he who eats my flesh and drinks my blood has eternal life, and I will raise him up at the last day. For my flesh is food indeed, and my blood is drink indeed. He who eats my flesh and drinks my blood abides in me, and I in him'" (John 6:51-56, RSV).

● ● ●

"Having purified your souls by your obedience to the truth for a sincere love of the brethren, love one another earnestly from the heart. You have been born anew, not of perishable seed but of imperishable, through the living and abiding word of God" (1 Peter 1:22-23, RSV). O the depth of the riches and wisdom and knowledge of God! How unsearchable are his judgments and how inscrutable his ways! From him and through him and to him are all things. To him be glory forever.

● ● ●

Communion Prayers

Prayer, of course, is a crucial part of the Communion observance. The leader will lead the group in the prayerful preparation for Communion in the beginning and lead the people in the proper consecrating experience at the end of the service.

The prayers of thanksgiving are most properly offered as the bread and the cup are to be received.

Prayers may be offered by the leader of the service, on occasion by lay leaders who are serving the elements, or may also be printed to be prayed in unison by the people or read and prayed silently.

Sometimes the prayers are pre- and post-Communion prayers, or they may be prayers for the bread and cup. Samples of these are shared here.

Pre-Communion Prayers

"O God, who by the life and death and rising again of thy dear Son hast consecrated for us a new and living way into the holiest of all, cleanse our minds, we beseech thee, by the inspiration of thy Holy Spirit, that drawing near unto thee with a pure heart and conscience undefiled, we may receive these thy gifts without sin, and worthily magnify thy holy Name; through Jesus Christ our Lord. Amen."[6]

● ● ●

"It is very meet, right, and our bounden duty that

we should at all times and in all places give thanks unto thee, O Lord, holy Father, almighty, everlasting God.

''Therefore with angels and archangels, and with all the company of heaven, we laud and magnify thy glorious name; evermore praising thee, and saying: Holy, holy, holy, Lord God of hosts, heaven and earth are full of thy glory. Glory be to thee, O Lord most high! Amen.''[7]

● ● ●

''O God, Father of our Lord Jesus Christ, who dost call us to draw near to thee in Holy Communion; look graciously, we beseech thee, upon thy servants who seek thy grace in this most holy ordinance. Give unto us true and hearty sorrow for past sins, power to confess the same unto thee, grace to seek thy mercy and forgiveness, and an earnest desire to walk before thee in newness and holiness of life; and mercifully grant that we, with all those who shall come to thy holy table, may be filled with thy Spirit in the inner man; that drawing near with penitent hearts and lively faith, we may receive the holy sacrament to our present and everlasting comfort; through thy Son, our Saviour, Jesus Christ. Amen.''[8]

Post-Communion Prayers

''Grant, O Lord, that the ears which have heard the voice of thy songs may be closed to the voice of clamor and dispute; that the eyes which have seen thy great love may also behold thy blessed hope; that the tongues which have sung thy praise may speak the truth; that the feet which have walked in thy courts may walk in the region of light; and that the souls of all who have received thy blessed sacrament may be restored to newness of life. Glory be to thee for thine unspeakable gift. Amen.''[9]

• • •

''Almighty and most gracious Father, who this day hast given Thy servants to remember the Lord Jesus in the sacrament of the Supper; grant that that mind which was in him may also be so formed in us that we may take upon us the burdens and duties which have been appointed us and follow in his steps, bearing contradiction patiently, subduing in ourselves every lawless and guilty desire, setting ourselves steadfastly against every evil work, and by our willing services and sacrifices bringing comfort and hope to those who are distressed; through our Savior Jesus Christ. Amen.''[10]

For the Bread

Glory and praise be to you, O God, our Father. In your tender mercy you gave your only Son, Jesus Christ our Lord, to suffer upon the cross for us. Grant us your Holy Spirit and sanctify us and this bread that it may be for us spiritual food. May we feed in our hearts on Him, our Savior and Lord.[11]

• • •

Dear Father of Light in whom there is no darkness, send us light for our souls lest we wander in darkness forever. We are gathered together at your dear Son's invitation. May this bread be to us a visible token of our fellowship with him.

• • •

O God who has broken the Bread of Life for a hungry world, help us to be hungry for this spiritual nourishment now. We bless you for this table that brings us together to receive the token of the manna from heaven. Make us feel the majesty of this Communion, and help us to go from this table cheered by your eternal presence and fed by the Christ.

• • •

Most holy and merciful Father, we are drawn to this table today to celebrate Jesus Christ, your Son and our Savior. We approach this Communion in humility and hope. Feed us today with this bread of life. May our spirits be nourished by this bread of heaven.

For the Cup

Dear Lord, help us now as we receive the cup, the symbol of your shed blood, to be properly grateful and ever humble. We acknowledge you died for us, and we are drawn closer to the cross and its meaning. From these realizations may we be more diligent in our service to you and more devoted to your truth. Bless us as we partake of this cup. Amen.

• • •

We thank you, O God, for the cup, symbol of the shed blood of your precious Son. We remember the supper, his cross, and his resurrection. We look forward to the fulfillment of his promise to eat and drink with us again in the coming kingdom. Let this cup be the cup of salvation as we trust in him and then a cup of fellowship as we drink with him. Amen.[12]

• • •

Grant us, O God, your presence as we receive the cup representing the blood of Jesus Christ shed for sinners such as we. May we receive him and the life that was in him as we drink of this sacred cup. May we be faithful to the vows we have taken to remember him and serve him. Amen.

• • •

Make ready, O God, our hearts to receive this symbolic cup. May we share the love and mercy poured into this cup as Jesus gave his life for us. Help us rejoice in the assurance that we are so loved. May we dedicate ourselves anew to living the life he calls us to live. We pray in his name. Amen.

Personal or Private Prayer at the Communion

Help me, O God, my Father, to remember the Lord, to understand the meaning of his love, his life, and his death for me. Take from my heart every doubt and fear and give me assurance of your forgiveness. May the Lord Jesus draw me nearer to you and to all my family and associates. Dear God, I commit myself to you; I'm open to your guidance and instructions. I pray for all who have special needs this day and for all my brothers and sisters in Christ. Amen.

• • •

I pray for myself today, O Lord. I ask for your mercy and your grace that I might know the gift of your peace. Help me resist the evil that continuously threatens. I am unable to be or do as I feel you will. Today, let your Holy Spirit give me true joy and a quiet mind. Have mercy upon me; protect me. As I take the bread and cup today, may Christ become more real to me than he has ever been, and may I be closer to him than ever. Let me have his assurance of eternal life even now. Amen.

• • •

I thank you, Lord, for this Holy Communion service. May I be strengthened for daily service to you. May my Christian witness be strengthened that I might inspire others. Let the life which was in Christ now be in me, and may I live that others might see him in me. May Christ's love, compassion, sympathies, and sensitivities become alive in me. Let the bread and the cup transform my thinking and living. Amen.

Prayers in Departing

We praise you and thank you, O God, for the privilege to have been at your table. We are grateful for the Communion. Now as we go into the world may your grace accompany us, may your peace be our blessing, and may your kingdom's interest receive our first loyalty. Through Jesus Christ our Lord. Amen.

• • •

Thank you, Lord, for the renewal of vision, faith, life, fellowship, and purpose which this service of Communion has afforded us. Send all of us out as workers in your vineyards to extend your kingdom in the world. Have your own way with us. To you be glory and praise now and forevermore. Amen.

• • •

Lord God, thank you for your presence around the table. Thank you for the bread of life shared with us; thank you for giving our thirsty souls to drink. Send us now into the world that we may minister to others and find the joy of our lives in Christ Jesus. Help us hear the cries for help; and heed our opportunities to give wherever there is need, even as Jesus would. Amen.

Words of Participation

These words are spoken by the leader at the appropriate times in the service when all are to eat and drink simultaneously. Sometimes these words are printed and the people read them silently and then partake.

Bread

"The body of our Lord Jesus Christ, which was given for thee, preserve thy soul and body unto everlasting life. Take and eat this in remembrance that Christ died for thee, and feed on him in thy heart by faith with thanksgiving."[13]

• • •

Let us eat of this bread in remembrance of Christ, and may the life which was in him be in us also.

• • •

"The bread which we break, is it not a participation in the body of Christ?" (1 Corinthians 10:16*b*, RSV). Take and eat.

• • •

Jesus shared many things with his disciples: prayer,

hardship, danger, love, forgiveness, healing, food. He broke the bread and gave to them, signifying his broken body.

●　●　●

This broken bread symbolizes Christ sharing with us his glory, truth, life, joy, love, and labor. The bread speaks to us of his humiliation there.

●　●　●

As you take this bread, be reminded of him whose body was broken and realize the suffering which shall redeem the world in our time. Eat of this bread.

●　●　●

"This is that bread which came down from heaven: not as your fathers did eat manna, and are dead: he that eateth of this bread shall live for ever" (John 6:58).

●　●　●

"And as they were eating, [Jesus] took bread, and when he had blessed, he brake it, and gave to them, and said, Take ye: this is my body" (Mark 14:22, ASV).

●　●　●

"As they were eating, he took a loaf, and after the blessing he broke and gave it to them, saying, 'Take this, it means my body'" (Mark 14:22, Moffatt).

●　●　●

"I am the living bread which came down from heaven: if any man eat of this bread, he shall live for ever: and the bread that I will give is my flesh, which I will give for the life of the world" (John 6:51).

●　●　●

"Jesus said, 'This is my body, which is given for you.'

Take and eat this in remembrance that Christ died for you, and feed on him in your heart by faith, with thanksgiving.''[14]

Cup

''The blood of our Lord Jesus Christ, which was shed for thee, preserve thy soul and body unto everlasting life. Drink this in remembrance that Christ's blood was shed for thee, and be thankful.''[15]

• • •

The Lord Jesus shed his life's blood for us to preserve us unto everlasting life; drink of it.

• • •

''The cup of blessing which we bless, is it not a participation in the blood of Christ?'' (1 Corinthians 10:16a, RSV). Take and drink.

• • •

''Jesus said, 'This cup is the new covenant in my blood, which is shed for you.' Drink this in remembrance that Christ died for you, and be thankful.''[16]

• • •

As we partake of the cup, we not only ask for forgiveness for our sins; but we also witness to the world that we believe with all our hearts that Jesus Christ is Lord. His blood, as represented in this cup, is our atonement.

• • •

As we lift the cup to our lips, let it reveal to our thirsting souls the greatness of his spirit whose soul was meek and lowly. May a like spirit be breathed into us. Drink of it.

• • •

"And according to the law, I may almost say, all things are cleansed with blood, and apart from the shedding of blood there is no remission" (Hebrews 9:22, ASV).

• • •

Let us drink of this cup in remembrance of Christ, and may the Spirit in which he died be our spirit.

• • •

"And he took a cup, and when he had given thanks, he gave it to them saying, 'Drink of it, all of you; for this is my blood of the covenant, which is poured out for many for the forgiveness of sins'" (Matthew 26:27-28, RSV).

• • •

At the end of the meal Jesus took the cup and said, "This cup stands for the new relation with God made possible at the cost of my death. You must continue to do this as often as you drink it to make you remember me."

• • •

Scripture: 1 Corinthians 10:16

• • •

"Know ye not that . . . ye are not your own? For ye are bought with a price . . . " (1 Corinthians 6:19-20), even the precious blood of Christ.

Words of Conclusion

Before the Communion hymn and following the moments of prayer and consecration, the observance can be concluded by any of the following final words:

"The earth is the LORD'S and the fulness thereof; the world, and they that dwell therein" (Psalm 24:1). We all belong to God. We all are objects of Christ's redeeming love.

● ● ●

"Having purified your souls by your obedience to the truth for a sincere love of the brethren, love one another earnestly from the heart" (1 Peter 1:22, RSV).

● ● ●

"You have been born anew, not of perishable seed but of imperishable, through the living and abiding word of God" (1 Peter 1:23, RSV).

● ● ●

After our Lord and his disciples ate the bread and drank the cup, it is said that they sang a hymn and went out. Let us likewise conclude our services.

● ● ●

Every time you eat this loaf and drink this cup you are publicly proclaiming the Lord's death until he comes again. (See 1 Corinthians 11:26.)

● ● ●

"Let your light so shine before men, that they may see your good works, and glorify your Father which is in heaven" (Matthew 5:16).

● ● ●

"Now unto him that is able to keep you from falling, and to present you faultless before the presence of his glory with exceeding joy, to the only wise God our Saviour, be glory and majesty, dominion and power, both now and ever. Amen" (Jude 24, 25).

• • •

"O give thanks unto the LORD; call upon his name; make known his deeds among the people" (Psalm 105:1).

• • •

Let us now depart with the hope of God in our eyes and the fire of his love in our hearts. May the presence of the Lord be felt by you as you depart. Be assured of his forgivenesss and receive his assurance of Eternal Life. May you witness to his love and grace and power.

• • •

"I beseech you therefore, brethren, by the mercies of God, that ye present your bodies a living sacrifice, holy, acceptable unto God, which is your reasonable service" (Romans 12:1).

• • •

"God is able to make all grace abound toward you; that ye, always having sufficiency in all things, may abound to every good work" (2 Corinthians 9:8).

• • •

Everyone who partakes of the bread and cup pledges oneself to share God's love with others. Herein is the hope of the world. Every one's search for salvation must become the responsibility of our souls. Only thus can the kingdom of God come to pass upon the earth.

• • •

Scripture: Colossians 3:1-10

Creeds and Statements

Many congregations that do not have creeds find it helpful to utilize creeds or statements of faith in the

Communion service to help people realize what we do believe. Samples are included here. To write a summary of what the congregation believes is a good project for a study group and this statement would be worthwhile to include in the Communion service.

A Brief General Statement

"We believe in God the Father, infinite in wisdom, power, and love, whose mercy is over all his works, and whose will is ever directed to his children's good.

"We believe in Jesus Christ, Son of God and Son of man, the gift of the Father's unfailing grace, the ground of our hope, and the promise of our deliverance from sin and death.

"We believe in the Holy Spirit as the divine presence in our lives, whereby we are kept in perpetual remembrance of the truth of Christ, and find strength and help in time of need.

"We believe that this faith should manifest itself in the service of love as set forth in the example of our blessed Lord, to the end that the Kingdom of God may come upon the earth. Amen."[17]

The Apostles' Creed

"I believe in God the Father Almighty, Maker of heaven and earth; and in Jesus Christ his only Son our Lord; who was conceived by the Holy Ghost, born of the Virgin Mary, suffered under Pontius Pilate, was crucified, dead, and buried; the third day he rose again from the dead: he ascended into heaven, and sitteth at the right hand of God the Father Almighty; from thence he shall come to judge the quick and the dead. I believe in the Holy Ghost, the holy catholic Church, the communion of saints, the forgiveness of sins, the resurrection of the body, and the life everlasting. Amen.''

A Scriptural Confession of Faith

''God is a spirit, and they that worship him must worship him in spirit and in truth. God is light and in him is no darkness at all, neither shadow that is cast by turning. God is love, and every one that loveth is begotten of God and knoweth God. Love never faileth, and there is no fear in love, but perfect love casteth out fear. So then we are debtors not to the flesh to live after the flesh, but we received the spirit of adoption whereby we cry Abba, Father. Being therefore always of good courage, we walk by faith, not by sight, and we make it our aim to be well pleasing unto him. For we know that, to them that love God, all things work together for good. And the peace of God, which passeth all understanding shall guard our hearts and our thoughts in Christ Jesus. Amen.''[18]

A Creed in New Testament Language

''We believe that God is a spirit, and they that worship him must worship him in spirit and in truth.

''We believe that God is universal, and that He has made of one blood all nations of men to dwell on the face of the whole earth in harmony.

''We believe that God is love, and everyone that

loves is born of God and knows God.

"We believe that Jesus is the Son of God, and as many as are led by the spirit of God, are sons of God.

"We believe that Jesus Christ is the redeemer of the world, and that God has given us eternal life, and this life is in His Son.

"We believe that where two or three are gathered in Christ's name, He is there in their midst, and they have fellowship with each other.

"We believe that the Lord Jesus is the way, the truth and the life.

"We believe that if we confess our sins, God is faithful and just, and will forgive our sins and cleanse us from all unrighteousness.

"We believe that the world will pass away, and the lust thereof; but He that does the will of God abides forever. Amen. Therefore we covenant to seek the advancement by the kingdom of God through public worship and private devotion, the preaching and teaching of the Gospel, consistent Christian living, personal evangelism and missionary endeavor."[19]

A Short Creed

"We believe in the Fatherhood of God and the Brotherhood of Man. We believe that Christ is the Way and the Truth and the Life. We believe in the clean heart, the unworldly life and the service of love which Jesus taught and exemplified. We accept his spirit and his teachings and seek to carry forward his unfinished work."[20]

OTHER INNOVATIONS

S ometimes people will leave a Communion service sharing the comment "Thank you, I really needed the Communion today." Often this feeling will be the result of introducing a new element to the service that has made the total experience of Communion more meaningful. To make the service memorable requires some innovation and planning. Consider some possibilities.

Consider the Communion as the major message of the service. Often we feel that the message must be the sermon, but this is not necessary. Let the sharing of a well-planned order of service make its own impact.

Music is a vital part of the service and can be better utilized than many services do at present. As the elements are distributed or as the people come forward, the congregation can sing softly a familiar hymn, such as "Amazing Grace," or "What a Friend," or some of the songs that are used at retreats or camps, such as "They Will Know We Are Christians by Our Love," or "Kum Ba Yah." The choir may sing a stanza of an appropriate hymn as distribution is made. Utilization of musical instruments in addition to the organ can be meaningful. The music of a violin, flute, or guitar can be very moving.

Participation of lay persons in the service is most appropriate. Lay people can serve as readers, lead in prayer, etc. Sometimes the ladies of the women's group may serve the Communion. Young people may also take part in the service, making a lasting impression on them as well as the congregation.

Since confession, absolution, and reconciliation are such integral parts of the Communion, some churches have incorporated plans such as having people write down failings or sins on slips of paper and place them on the table or burn them in a receptacle on the table. The acts of ''passing the peace'' or giving each other Scripture words of assurance can also be meaningful. A suggested ''passing the peace'' is as follows: clasp the hand of the person next to you and say, ''(name of person), I celebrate your life, the peace of Christ be with you.''

Some ministers will have the congregation say in unison the words of participation before taking the elements. To have the participants say together ''This is my body, broken for you'' can be moving.

Some churches have found it helpful to have the congregation come forward a segment at a time and kneel in front and be served, or have them file by the table and take their own elements back to their pews. Sometimes families will be asked to come as families and be served, with singles coming with a friend. It is good to vary the method of serving.

Sometimes, especially at services other than Sunday mornings, the use of a common loaf or a single chalice can be inspiring and help people sense our oneness in the common loaf and cup. The minister might want to consider passing a dish of salt to the communicants at the close of a service, asking the people to take just a pinch into the palm of their hand and, when all have been served, telling the people that as they leave they should remember, in the words of Matthew 5:13, that they are to be the "salt of the earth," living effective Christian lives.

The minister can announce a family Communion and ask that all the members of the family sit together. Family-oriented Scripture, music, and meditation can be used, and when time for serving the bread and cup comes, the servers can direct families as a unit to kneel at the front or to sit on the front pew and be served. Special attention must be paid to singles.

Many of our churches have two major ordinances, baptism and Communion. These can both be observed very effectively in the same service as the new Christians are welcomed and served their first Communion.

All the special days observed by the nation as well as the church are occasions for special Communion observances: Memorial Day, Independence Day, Thanksgiving, even Valentine's Day.

Observing Communion in different places is often effective, such as on the church lawn, in an upper room at the church, in the fellowship hall, etc. Communion can be served effectively in the hospital room, at the funeral home, in prison, in a private home on special occasions, etc.

Imagination and sensitivity are keys to making the Communion worship more and more memorable for participants, including the pastor.

Small Group Communion

The people are assembled around tables at which there is a small loaf of bread, a cup, and a salt shaker. A lay leader will be at each table.

The minister calls the service together and reads Scripture to illustrate the oneness and the fellowship we have in Christ. A brief exposition of the theme may be made.

After prayer the group participates. Along with the minister, the lay leader breaks the loaf and passes it on. Then the minister directs them to eat.

After a period of silent prayer the theme of forgiveness and assurance can be reviewed in Scripture and discussed as preparation to receive the cup.

As with the bread, the pastor blesses the contents as he lifts the cup high, then sips from it, and passes it on. The lay leaders follow him.

The pastor then calls attention to the salt on the table and reviews for them the importance of each person going into the world to represent Christ. The pastor reads appropriate Scripture and then demonstrates putting some salt on the back of the hand and tasting it to illustrate its effectiveness.

Service of Preparation

In times past, the church had a special service of preparation for communicants. Sometimes this service was held during the week preceding Communion Sunday, a Sunday or midweek evening, or the hour before Communion was to be served.

The Jews believed they could not rush into the presence of God without preparation and purification of their minds and hearts; thus they participated in such a service. Christians who prepare for the service of Communion can likewise benefit greatly. Preparation of the mind and heart will consider the experiences of repentance, confession, humility, commitment, and consecration.

This service can be most beneficial to new and young Christians as the pastor instructs in the theology, symbolism, and disciplines associated with the Communion. Sometimes the service of preparation will be a time to cultivate the sense of community and fellowship. Reconciliation can be effected during this time of preparation.

This service also affords an opportunity for consecration and reverence for those who will be preparing the elements of the service as well as for those lay persons participating in the service. In the service there should be a time of prayer and dedication also for the pastor who will be in charge of the service.

The following outline could be used for this service:

Prelude (*everyone in silent prayer and meditation*)
Call to Worship: Micah 6:8
Invocation (*prayer for the Holy Spirit's presence*)
Hymn
Call to Confession

Confession Prayer (*unison*)
Words of Assurance
Old Testament Lesson
Hymn
New Testament Lesson
Meditation *(thoughts on some aspect
                of the Communion)*
Call to Self-Examination:
    responsive reading of the Beatitudes, with silence fol-
    lowing each verse
Words of Anticipation: from Luke 22:9-12
Hymn
Benediction
Postlude

NOTES

Chapter 1

[1]The term "Mass" is taken from the last words in the Roman liturgy: *"ite, missa est."* It was originally a dismissal of the people at the close of the teaching part of the worship service, and later the term "mass" came to represent the entire service which was the sacrament or the Holy Mysteries.

Chapter 2

[1]Adapted from a prayer, source unknown.

[2]Adapted from a prayer, source unknown.

[3]From the hymn "I Heard the Voice of Jesus Say."

[4]From the Gregorian Sacramentary or *The Book of Common Prayer* (Nashville: Thomas Nelson, Inc., 1944), p. 6.

Chapter 3

[1]Robert F. Bishop, "His Friends and Enemies," *Church Management Magazine,* February, 1957, p. 49.

[2]From the Gregorian Sacramentary or *The Book of Common Prayer* (Nashville: Thomas Nelson, Inc., 1944), p. 67.

[3]*Ibid.,* p. 75.

[4]Adapted from the Traditional Service by the Waldenses from the thirteenth century.

[5]*The Book of Common Prayer,* p. 67.

Chapter 5

[1]Compiled and edited by James Dalton Morrison, *Minister's Service Book* (New York: Harper & Row, Publishers, Inc., 1937), pp. 113-114.

[2] *The Book of Worship for Church and Home* (New York: The Methodist Publishing House, 1944), p. 377. Copyright © 1952 by Pierce and Washabaugh (Abingdon Press). Used by permission.

[3] Quoted in James L. Christensen, *The Minister's Service Handbook* (Old Tappan, N.J.: Fleming H. Revell Company, 1960), pp. 31-32.

[4] M. K. W. Heicher, ed., *Ministers Manual* (New York: Harper & Row, Publishers, Inc., 1961), p. 37, adapted from an article in *World Outlook,* the mission publication of the United Methodist Church.

[5]From the hymn ''When I Survey the Wondrous Cross.''

[6]Liturgy of St. James.

[7]*The Book of Worship for Church and Home,* p. 53.

[8]Charles W. Merriam, *Church Worship Book* (Boston: The Pilgrim Press, 1931), p. 82.

[9]From the Liturgy of Malabar quoted in the *Minister's Service Book,* compiled and edited by James Dalton Morrison (New York: Harper & Row, Publishers, Inc., 1937), p. 125.

[10]Hugh Cameron quoted in *ibid.,* p. 124.

[11]Adapted from William Robinson, *The Administration of the Lord's Supper* (Birmingham: The Berean Press, 1959), pp. 43-44.

[12]*Ibid.,* p. 44.

[13]*The Book of Worship . . . ,* p. 386.

[14]*Ibid.,* p. 380.

[15]*Ibid.,* p. 386.

[16]*Ibid.,* p. 380.

[17]*Ibid.,* p. 11.

[18]Albert W. Palmer, ed., *Aids to Worship* (New York: Macmillan, Inc., 1944), p. 21.

[19]From the church worship bulletin of the Prince of Peace Church, Sacramento, California, October 5, 1975.

[20]Merriam, *op. cit.,* p. 24.